Devotions for Any Occasion

Jerry Hayner

Abingdon Press

Devotions for Any Occasion

Copyright © 1987 by Abingdon Press

All rights reserved.
No part of this work may be reproduced or transmitted in any form or by any means, electronic or mechanical, including photocopying and recording, or by any information storage or retrieval system, except as may be expressly permitted by the 1976 Copyright Act or in writing from the publisher. Requests for permission should be addressed to Abingdon Press, 201 Eighth Avenue South, P.O. Box 801, Nashville, TN 37202.

ISBN 0-687-10513-7

Scripture quotations designated GNB are from the *Good News Bible*, the Bible in Today's English version. Copyright © American Bible Society, 1976. Used by permission.

Scripture quotations designated KJV are from the King James, or Authorized, Version of the Bible.

Scripture quotations designated MLB are from THE MODERN LANGUAGE BIBLE: THE BERKELEY VERSION IN MODERN ENGLISH. Copyright © 1945, 1959, 1969 by Zondervan Publishing House. Used by permission.

Scripture quotations designated RSV are from the Revised Standard Version of the Bible, copyrighted 1946, 1952, © 1971, 1973 by the Division of Christian Education of the National Council of the Churches of Christ in the U.S.A., and are used by permission.

Devotions from page 21 to the end of the book are adapted from *Say Hello to Life*, also by Jerry Hayner, published by Broadman Press. Copyright © 1980 by Jerry Hayner.

94 95 96 97 98 99 00 01 02 03 04 — 10 9 8 7 6

MANUFACTURED IN THE UNITED STATES OF AMERICA

Contents

Struggle . . . a Gift from God 4
One String at a Time 5
You Are Expensive 6
All Things New 7
"I Love You" 8
"If I Were . . ." 9
A Thankful Heart 10
The Simple Life 11
In Spite of Our Dirt 12
God: A Voice for All 13
God Has the Last Word 14
Mind Over Matter 15
What's Your "Handle"? 16
Patience and Encouragement 17
How Beautiful the World *Could* Be 18
Channeling Anger 19
The Great Change Agent 20
Running Life's Race 21
Erasers 22
What's Your Name? 23
God's Gifts 24
Could We Be Friends? 25
God Never Lets Go 26
Consider the Turtle 27
Taking Off Our Masks 28
Starting Over . . . with God 29
Waiting 30
Rest in the Lord 31
Loneliness 32
Let Us Not Be Weary 33
Let Go and Let God 34
Get Well, Soon 35
God *Is* for Us 36
Comfort One Another 37
The Story of My Life 38
Friend or Enemy? 39
A Meaningful Life 40
"Likes" from "Lacks" 41
God's Enabling Love 42
Self-appreciation 43
Making Decisions 44
Are You Listening? 45
Blessed Interruptions 46
Under Our Skin 47
A Little Kinder Than Necessary 48

Struggle . . . a Gift from God

Hymn Suggestions: "Come, Ye Disconsolate";
"From Every Stormy Wind That Blows"

Struggle is a word many dislike. It speaks of hardship, pain, suffering, and spent energy. Therefore, many of us resist struggle. We don't like it. We might even desire our successes to come with a minimum amount of struggle. Yet, life is not made that way, is it?

I once heard of a little boy who decided to help a butterfly emerge from its cocoon. When the movement began inside the cocoon, the boy carefully enlarged the hole through which the butterfly was to emerge. This made the butterfly's entrance into the world an easier one.

The butterfly made its appearance without much of a struggle—the only problem was that it could not fly. Butterflies gain strength in their wings by pushing against the sides of the cocoon. There was no need for that, so there was no development of the wings.

Parents sometimes make life too easy for their children. We make their decisions for them. We try to shield them from danger. We insulate them from trouble as best we can. Some of them grow up unable to fly. They have not learned to struggle.

Paul said, "We also boast of our troubles, because we know that trouble produces endurance, endurance brings God's approval, and his approval creates hope" (Romans 5:3-4 GNB).

Struggle might be God's gift to you. God is with you. Don't quit. Perhaps you're being trained to "fly."

Lord, I confess I would like to have life a little easier than it sometimes is. Sometimes I think my wings are strong enough. Assure me of your presence in the midst of my struggles, and so shall I endure. Amen.

Galatians 6:9

One String at a Time

Hymn Suggestions: "God Will Take Care of You";
"He Hideth My Soul"

In *Gulliver's Travels,* there is the time when Gulliver finds himself washed ashore on a strange little island that he learns is called Lilliput. The land is occupied by very small people who are no larger than his thumb. Because he is overcome with exhaustion following his shipwreck, Gulliver falls asleep on the beach. The little people who discover him are afraid because of his size, so they tie him to the ground. When he awakes, he finds himself helpless—tied down by hundreds of little strings.

Are there any "little strings" that you have immobilized? It doesn't take much to limit the magnificent human organism. A little sickness, a little fatigue, a little word someone carelessly spoke, and all of a sudden we are wiped out. How many days are ruined? How much good might have been done? Nothing good happened, because the little strings made us helpless.

Life is like a lot of little strings. We are sometimes bound by the strings of the past, of the present, and of the future. We struggle with the braided rope that holds us back. We can't handle all of it at once, but we can handle our struggles and trials if we deal with them one at a time.

Jesus said, "Do not worry about tomorrow; it will have enough worries of its own. There is no need to add to the troubles each day brings" (Matthew 6:34 GNB). Break one string at a time. Don't let life tie you to the ground. God will help you.

Lord, so often I let the little things in life tie me down. I worry and fret over yesterday's spilt milk or tomorrow's unseen problem. Help me to live one day at a time with the strength and help you offer. Amen.

Deuteronomy 33:25

You Are Expensive

Hymn Suggestions: "I Hear Thy Welcome Voice";
"O Thou God of My Salvation"

Have you ever felt that you didn't matter to anyone? All of us want to matter; it's a fundamental characteristic of our human nature. Even babies have instinctive ways of getting the attention they desire. As we move toward the twilight years of life, one of our greatest fears is that of being insignificant. From the cradle to the grave, we face the reality of wanting to be significant.

Some think, "I'll get rich; then I'll be noticed." Some say, "I'll do something really big; it matters not whether it is good or bad, but I'll get attention." We have our ways of getting attention—we dress or undress; we work hard at our professions; we study; we play. We do lots of things to make people notice us.

Yet, in spite of it all, some of us have that abysmal feeling that we aren't important. We feel as if we could disappear from society, and no one would miss us.

Listen to these words:

> When I look at the sky, which you have made,
>   at the moon and the stars,
>   which you set in their places—
> what is man, that you think of him;
>   mere man, that you care for him?
> Yet you made him inferior only to yourself;
>   you crowned him with glory and honor.
>   (Psalm 8:3-5 GNB)

God has made all of us significant. *God never made no junk!* Remember that the next time you feel like a zero. Remember that Jesus died for you. You are very expensive.

Lord, when I am tempted to think of myself as a nobody, help me to remember that you have made me significant by creation and by redemption. May I see myself through your eyes. In Jesus' name, I pray, amen.

Matthew 10:31

All Things New

Hymn Suggestions: "Jesus Is All the World to Me"; "Look, Ye Saints!"

More than one person would like to be able to turn back the hands of time, back to a day that used to be, back to a time that maybe never was, but just seemed to be. We'd like to go back to before a decision was made, to before a loss was felt, to before a word was spoken.

How can one begin again? The life-cycle of a butterfly is an interesting study. At one time the butterfly was nothing more than a caterpillar in a cocoon. In its dark cave something happened to the lowly worm. Wings were formed and delicately painted. A metamorphosis, a change of life, transpired.

Can something like that happen to us? Not exactly like that, but we can begin again. We can go beyond our past. Jesus called it a "new birth." I cannot explain it any more than I can explain what takes place in the darkness of a cocoon, but I know something happens. People who have given up on themselves and on life suddenly have renewed hope. Attitudes change. God performs a work of grace in a person's spirit.

About her blindness, Helen Keller once said, "I do not understand it, but I have learned the overcoming of it." Why should one want to go backward when one can go forward? Why should one long for yesterday when there is the newness of today and tomorrow? Our God is One who can make all things new—even us. Believe it and be blessed.

Father of time and eternity, we long for a place and a time when life was more serene and simple. We know we can't go back. Help us to go forward with faith, hope, and love. Amen.

II Corinthians 5:17

"I Love You"

Hymn Suggestions: "I Love Thee";
"I Will Sing the Wondrous Story"

For his hilarious little book, *Dear Pastor,* Bill Adler selected letters children wrote to their pastors. One such letter catches the eye: "Dear Pastor, i know God loves me but i wish he would give me an 'A' on my report card so i could be sure. Love, Theresa, age 8, Milwaukee."

If you can't identify with those feelings, then you and I are not coming from the same place. There have been times when I have wanted God to do something special, something right now, just "so I could be sure" of his love.

We're like that with one another, aren't we? We like up-to-date, fresh expressions of someone's love. We need new encouragement and affirmation. Yesterday's love won't compensate for today's need.

I suppose we'll always be that way to some degree. The fact that something good happened in the past is all right, but it's not as good as having something good happen in the present.

Put the shoe on the other foot. If we want to receive some fresh assurance of someone's love—even God's—how are we doing in giving fresh assurance ourselves? Has God heard from you lately? Has he heard of your love and devotion?

And what about other people? Is there someone who would like to hear you say, "I love you"? Is there a phone call you should make, or a letter you should write? It's O.K. to receive assurance of love. It's O.K. to give it, too.

Father, give us the desire on this day to go out of our way to make life a little brighter, a little better, and a little easier for someone else, for Jesus' sake. Amen.

I John 4:7

"If I Were..."

Hymn Suggestions: "The Way of the Cross Leads Home"; "At Calvary"

Most of us have some idea of what we might do if we were somebody else. It is a favorite armchair game we play: "If I were you...." "If I were the coach...." "If I were God...." We have all the answers. We would do a better job than that which is being done.

"If I were...." So much time is lost thinking about what we might do—if. But life doesn't turn on *if;* it makes its way on the wheels of *since* and *because.*

Each one must accept the reality of one's situation and spend less time in doing another's task. The truth is that you and I don't really know what we would do if we were in another's shoes. We don't have the information or the feelings of other people. We don't have the responsibility. We don't see the whole scene.

If we are to live our lives successfully, there are some things we must do. First, we must accept the fact that we are who we are and not someone else. We must work within our possibilities and limitations.

Second, we must be more understanding of others. Until one walks a mile in the shoes of another, that one cannot fully appreciate the actions of the other. We can offer encouragement and suggestions to another, but we cannot presume that we have the last word.

Third, we can surrender ourselves and others to God. It is he who can help us all.

Lord, you came to earth to feel our pain, to understand our heartaches, and to endure our temptation. As you entered our skin and identified with us, so may we try harder to understand the situations of others. In Jesus' name, amen.

Galatians 6:2

A Thankful Heart

Hymn Suggestions: "Count Your Blessings";
"Now Thank We All Our God"

I have never had much difficulty thanking someone for the good gifts of life. It has come as no hardship for me to thank loved ones and friends for their love and self-giving that have made my life more enjoyable. I find it easy to thank God for the truly good and perfect gifts he gives to me.

Then I read about Hans Lilje. He was a German by ancestry and an American by birth who was taken as a prisoner of war during World War II. In a concentration camp, he was abused and severely mistreated. Yet, he never failed to thank the guard after the malicious beatings he took.

"Why do you thank me?" once asked the guard.

"You're doing your duty, aren't you?" responded the injured Lilje. "Then I am thanking you for being obedient to your superiors." His attitude of gratitude changed the treatment he and his fellow prisoners received.

It isn't easy for us to be thankful for the painful experiences or treatment we receive in life. Bitterness is much better, we think. Yet, life is not made better by bitterness, but by a spirit of gratitude.

Gratitude enables us to overcome self-pity, anger, hatred, and even resentment toward God. Paul said, "Don't worry about anything, but in all your prayers ask God for what you need, always asking him with a thankful heart" (Phil. 4:6 GNB). Bitterness is easy, but gratitude is better.

Lord, in the midst of the pain and suffering of life, give us the grace of gratitude. May our minds be so thankful for the peace we have with you that all of the troubles of life will pale in comparison. Through Jesus we pray, amen.

Psalm 92:1-4

The Simple Life

Hymn Suggestions: "Where Cross the Crowded Ways of Life"; "Near to the Heart of God"

The psalmist said, "The Lord preserveth the simple." That is a timely word to both his generation and ours. In a society that is highly mechanized and complicated, in which everything runs by the computer and the clock, in which people hardly have time to enjoy the finer things of life, we need simplicity.

A poet said, "Little we see in nature that is ours." That is unfortunate, for there is much in nature that could speak soothingly to our jangled nerves. Jesus looked at nature and was comforted to think that a lily could survive beautifully without anxiety.

Far too many of us are living life-styles that are too complicated for our own good. Husbands and wives have no time for each other. Parents and children wave at one another in passing—if they are still speaking. Neighbors don't know the names of neighbors. We're just too busy.

I heard of a man who one morning used two shaving brushes instead of one and saved seventeen seconds. Next morning, he used two razors instead of one and saved additional seconds. On the third morning, he lost two minutes patching up his chin, which had been sliced by two razors.

The simple life—that is what we need. Time to smell the roses and to pet a dog. Time to be alone with the Master and to reflect on his love and goodness. We need to simplify life so that we can enjoy it more. How is your schedule today?

Dear Jesus, you had time—time to do what needed to be done, time for children, and time for yourself. You spent time with your friends and time with your Father. Help us learn to use time and to make it a friend. Teach us, Lord. Amen.

Ephesians 5:16

In Spite of Our Dirt

Hymn Suggestions: "I Am Thine, O Lord";
"Let Others See Jesus in You"

In *The Diary of a Country Priest,* George Bernanos told of the cleaning lady who had the responsibility of keeping the church building presentable. She worked so hard at her job that she became ill and died. Bernanos said, "The mistake she made wasn't to fight dirt, sure enough, but to try to do away with it altogether. As if that were possible! A parish is bound to be dirty. A whole Christian society's a lot dirtier. You wait for the judgment day and see what the angels'll be sweeping out of even the most saintly monasteries!"

No one is perfect, so we make a grave mistake in expecting perfection of others, or of ourselves, for that matter. That doesn't mean that we shouldn't try to be the very best we can be in behavior and performance. It's easy to take consolation in the fact that "nobody's perfect" and thus excuse our indiscretions and failings.

It is also easy to make the mistake of expecting too much from others and thus opening ourselves for a disappointment when that one fails to reach our expectations. There will always be dirt. People will have dust and dirt on them, and so will we.

We must learn to accept our humanity and that of others. We are sinners one and all. Our gratitude is to the One who forgives our sins and cleanses us from our trespasses. He loves and accepts us in spite of our dirt and gives us the capacity to do the same with others.

O Lord of Righteousness, thank you for loving us as unrighteous as we are. Make us clean, and help us to love the unclean ones. Perhaps through that love we can lead them to you, the Perfect One. Amen.

Romans 3:23

God: A Voice for All

Hymn Suggestions: "All Things Bright and Beautiful";
"Gentle Jesus, Meek and Mild"

A song has the lyrics, "Bless the beasts and the children, for in this world they have no voice, they have no choice." Have you ever wondered about those who fit that description—no voice, no choice?

Not all of them are deaf mutes. Some can hear quite well, maybe too well. They hear all those harsh, critical, condemning words that are leveled at them. When they try to speak, to defend themselves, to express themselves, they are cut off with the anger of one who says, "I don't care what you think. . . ."

All around us are people who are limited in life because of poor self-images. For so long they have been beaten down and hurt by insensitive and uncaring people. For so long they have missed out on the blessings of love, care, compassion, and consideration. Some of them are adult children, aren't they?

Jesus cared for the so-called "little people" of life, those whom life seemingly had passed by and left behind—beggars alongside the roadways; children scrambling through the streets; the lame who could not work for their living; and the blind, who always seemed to stumble and fall. He even cared for the sinners, whose lives were so messed up that no one wanted them around.

How do you treat the hurting ones? How Christlike are you?

For all the hurting people, dear God, give us compassion and love. For all the unblessed ones, give us the capacity to be a blessing. Through him who blessed us all, amen.

Matthew 19:14

God Has the Last Word

Hymn Suggestions: "The Head That Once Was Crowned"; "Majestic Sweetness Sits Enthroned"

Many people do not enjoy life because of death. That is true at two very important junctures: First, we are not able to get death out of life, and second, we sometimes can't get life out of death.

Look at the problem of getting death out of life. Fear of death, or continual awareness of it, can keep one from experiencing life at its best. One is afraid of drowning, so swimming is never tried. One is afraid of being killed in a plane crash, so air travel is eliminated. The fear of death is so strong that life is lived in death's ominous shadow. One sees the thorns behind the roses, so one does not enjoy the fragrance of the flower.

On the other hand, some of us cannot get life out of death. We find it difficult to remove ourselves from some painful loss. It might have been the death of a dear loved one, a divorce, the loss of an ability or a job, or something that was devastating at the time.

How do we get death out of life and life out of death? First, we must believe in a God who is "the resurrection and the life." It is he who enables us to overcome. Second, we must accept the fact that to live is to experience death someday. That should make us neither foolhardy nor timid.

Death is always with us in some form, but God is with us, too. Men made a cross, but God made an empty tomb. He has the last word. Surrender your fears and losses to him.

Lord, death is frightening. It is something we constantly fight against; we don't like to think about it. Give us such a strong assurance of your love and power that death will have no control over us. Amen.

Romans 8:38-39

Mind Over Matter

Hymn Suggestions: "The Rock That Is Higher Than I"; "In the Hour of Trial"

I once read about a mother who came up with a great idea for keeping her four-year-old son out of the cookies and candy when she took him to the supermarket. Before entering the door, she took off his belt. He then kept his hands busy trying to keep his pants from falling down. I guess you could say he became preoccupied with something more important than candy.

"Mind over matter," we have been told over and over. What gets our attention will get our response. If we allow ourselves to become absorbed with pleasure in any of its forms, we will seek that pleasure. The mind has a tremendous capacity for controlling the eyes, the hands, and the total body.

How do we overcome our temptations? Perhaps part of the secret is in that which gets our attention. We must become preoccupied with something more important, something better.

Paul wrote: "Fill your minds with those things that are good and that deserve praise: things that are true, noble, right, pure, lovely, and honorable" (Phil. 4:8 GNB). The proverb writer said that what a person thinks is what that person really is.

We may not have much control over the temptations that can come our way, but we can choose our state of mind. Think about those things that are good, wholesome, and Christlike. So shall we have strength for the temptations.

Father in heaven, you gave us our minds. Let us use them to think your thoughts so that we might do your will and thus enjoy fullness of life. Amen.

Philippians 2:2-3

What's Your "Handle"?

Hymn Suggestions: "Abide With Me";
"Open My Eyes That I May See"

"How can anyone have faith in this kind of world?" Have you ever wondered that? Lots of people have. Some will openly express their bewilderment. Others will quietly doubt, fearing that they will not appear as spiritual as others.

I can identify with those people who are frustrated with failure, their own or that of others. They see so much evil that seems to be unlimited, unhindered—yet rewarded—and wonder why heaven is so silent. Indeed, how can one have faith in this kind of world?

There are "handles" we try to hold onto in order to gain our answer. For some, a handle is money and what it can do; money symbolizes power, security, and the life of ease. For others, education is a handle. Knowledge gained can enable us to get certain positions in life. We are equipped to cope with the vast unknown.

People are handles to which some may try to hold. Have you not known people who have built their lives around other people? Some lives may collapse when those handles are no longer there.

Is there something to which I can cling? "And now abideth faith, hope, love . . . these three." They abide. They continue on and on—faith in God; hope that the future will be good; love for God, for self, for others. These are some good handles. The psalmist says that though the heart and body fail, yet God is my possession forever. What's your handle?

Everlasting Father, in a time when troubles are all around us, help us to find our security in the One who has been described as a sure foundation. Give us inner security based on our relationship with Christ. Amen.

John 14:1

Patience and Encouragement

Hymn Suggestions: "My Redeemer";
"My Savior's Love"

I stood in line waiting for the new cashier to complete her search for the price tags or the black computer marks on each product. Each item was searched for with care. Her faced showed signs of tension. It was her first day; the sign on the cash register advised: "Please Be Patient, New Clerk." There was some grumbling from the rear of the line. I hope she didn't hear the snide remarks that were being made.

I thought, "Why is it that we want everyone to be experts even when they're learning?" All of us have been beginners, and some of us are still beginners. In some ways, everyone is a beginner, because each new day presents fresh challenges, new problems, and new experiences. We should be patient with beginners; unfortunately, many of us are not.

In a new marriage, husbands and wives are often impatient with each other. Learning how to relate as a companion is not easy. Marriage is something new, something different. "Please Be Patient, New Husband, New Wife."

And what about the children? They make mistakes. They're not perfect, even as their parents aren't perfect. Is more patience needed for them?

Paul said, "And may God, the source of patience and encouragement, enable you to have the same point of view among yourselves by following the example of Christ Jesus" (Romans 15:5 GNB). Patience and encouragement—who doesn't need those things?

Father, as you so willingly and tenderly wait for your children to learn how to live the abundant life, so give us patience to wait for others. While we're waiting, let us learn to offer encouragement, too. Amen.

I Timothy 6:11

How Beautiful the World Could *Be*

Hymn Suggestions: "For the Beauty of the Earth";
"This Is My Father's World"

Reflecting back on his days in a German concentration camp during World War II, Victor Frankl told about a prisoner who came running into a building in which other prisoners were found huddled on the floor, eating their ration of soup. On their faces was the look of emptiness.

He begged them to go with him onto the assembly grounds to see the beautiful sunset God had painted on the evening sky. Its rich tones of red and violet seemed to be the bookends holding the pastel shades of blue, green, and orange. Puddles of water stood on the earth where a rain shower had left its mark. On those puddles one could see the sunset mirrored and shining. After several minutes of deep silence, one of the prisoners wistfully said, "How beautiful the world could be!"

Many people can say that. "My life would be beautiful if. . . ." "The place where I work, where I live, where I play could be beautiful if. . . ."

How beautiful the world could be if people were more tolerant of the weaknesses and frailties in one another. How beautiful the world could be if people were given the chance to change, to grow, to become what God meant them to be.

How beautiful the world could be if we were to take Jesus seriously and follow him more closely. Our way of living would improve as would our way of loving. How beautiful the world *could* be!

Father of all beauty, you gave us sunsets to show us a part of your radiant splendor. Help us try to make our days so full of love and joy that sunsets will serve only as the crowning touch on our evening sky. In Jesus' name, amen.

Psalm 19:1-2

Channeling Anger

Hymn Suggestions: "Savior, More Than Life to Me"; "More Like the Master"

Have you ever been so angry with someone that you nearly had to bite your tongue to keep from saying something harsh and ugly? Have you ever had to count to ten to calm your hostility? If so, then you can identify with the emotions Simon Peter felt on the day Jesus was arrested.

We are told that Simon Peter struck off with a sword the ear of the high priest's servant. Is there someone whose ear, or even head, you have thought about amputating? I hope you have never gotten that angry with anyone, but anger is a part of life, isn't it? There are times when it seems that "ear removals" might be the only way to adequately express our anger; maybe that is what it means to be human.

Perhaps there are few emotions more difficult to handle than anger. Anger indicates that something really matters. It means that we are taking people and life seriously. It isn't a sinful emotion, for the Bible tells us to "be angry and sin not."

If we are to "sin not" we must learn to channel our anger. At times we must walk away from that which creates it. At other times we must face the issue and deal with it openly, honestly, and with a deep desire to establish a better relationship with the one who has troubled us.

Let us surrender ourselves and our situations to God. He can help us properly handle our feelings of anger.

Father, I confess that I get angry at times, but I'm not ashamed of that. I am sometimes ashamed of the way my anger controls me rather than my being in control. Teach me to be angry and sin not. For Christ's sake, I pray, amen.

Proverbs 19:11

The Great Change Agent

Hymn Suggestions: "Let Jesus Come into Your Heart"; "Tell Me the Stories of Jesus"

Many of us look at our futures with the feeling that something has got to give, something has to be changed. It isn't an unusual feeling, because it isn't an unusual circumstance we might have.

Our problem is that we sometimes don't know how to go about making the desired change. Some would take the line of least resistance, but that isn't always good. Some drift with the stream; it's easier to give in to something than it is to try to control it.

Why do we have so much difficulty in making those changes that would make life better for ourselves and others? Is it because of failure in the past when we have tried to make changes? Is it because we don't really know what to do, what changes to make? Is it because we're tired of trying, and any change might require more effort from us?

God is the Great Change Agent; he is in the business of changing lives. The Bible reminds us that God can enter into the grimmest of circumstances and make something good of what he finds. Could he do the same for us? I think so.

Whatever change needs to be made in your life, think about it very carefully. Is it right? Is it good for you and others? Is it pleasing to God? If so, with the help of God, set your mind to it, work hard at it. The courage to change can be God's gift to you.

Lord, I thank you for the change you made in me when Jesus came to live in my heart. May I make whatever changes are necessary to accommodate his presence. Make life more meaningful for me, I pray. Amen.

Romans 8:28

Running Life's Race

Hymn Suggestions: "A Charge to Keep I Have";
                       "I Walk with the King"

"Don't let anyone get your goat!" Have you heard that expression? Do you know what it means? In days of yore it was common for farmers to own race horses. These horses, by their very natures, were animals that were nervous and high-strung. Someone discovered that putting a goat in the same stable with the race horse allowed the goat's sedate, calm manner to have a positive effect on the horse.

When there was to be a race between one farmer's horse and that of another, it became common practice for someone to try to steal the goat from a competitor's barn, leaving the horse alone through the night. The next day would find the horse not at its best in competition. "Don't let anyone get your goat" is supposed to be a statement originating from that setting.

We sometimes use that statement in reference to our relationships with other people: "Don't let them get your goat." "Don't let them get to you." "Don't let them get the best of you."

People "get our goat" with words they say to us and about us. They create high tension for us with the things they do to us or to those who are significant to us.

No one seemed to "get Jesus' goat"; he didn't let them. Even when things were tense and the race for men's souls was on the line, he kept his cool. If we were more like him, we would do a better job of running life's race.

Lord, teach us to be more tolerant of the things we do not like in others. Help us not to allow others to rob us of the joy and peace you desire us to have. Help us learn to live like our Lord. In his name, we pray. Amen.

Hebrews 12:1

Erasers

Hymn Suggestions: "In the Hour of Trial";
"Jesus, Savior, Pilot Me"

People who type for a living are always interested in the possibility of erasures, so onto the market came coarse erasers with bristly brushes on the end. Later, a liquid mistake remover was introduced; then came a filmy piece of paper that would remove mistakes when it was typed over. Now we have electronic typewriters and word processors that make erasures simple. Whether we type or write for a living, we're concerned about erasers; we know that sooner or later we are going to need them.

That's true of life, too, isn't it? All of us make mistakes. No one is perfect. Some don't worry about it; they just go on "typing" over the same mistake again and again. They really mess up their paper.

Others are more conscientious. They rub holes where the mistakes were. Sometimes their efforts at removing the errors look worse than the errors—you can overdo it, you know. God asks that we confess our sins and do what we can to correct the wrong, but we don't need to beat ourselves to death.

The eraser I am most grateful for is one that uses blood: "The blood of Jesus Christ, God's Son, cleanses us from all sin." Think of that! God has a way of removing our sins and leaving us with a clean sheet of paper. It is as if the sin were never committed. I like God's eraser the best. How about you?

Lord, I hate to make mistakes, but I make them over and over again, even on the same spots. You must get tired of erasing the same places. But even if you don't, Lord, help me to know that the power that erases is the same power that can prevent the mistake from being made. Let me trust you. Amen.

Psalm 103:11-12

What's Your Name?

Hymn Suggestions: "In Christ There Is No East or West"; "O Love That Wilt Not Let Me Go"

One day a man asked a little girl, "Which would you rather be called, 'Negro' or 'black'?" She calmly responded, "I'd rather be called 'Carrie.' " Of course, she would. Wouldn't you rather be known by your name instead of by some label? None of us should be ashamed of our race. When people call us by our names, they acknowledge the fact that we are not a race. Each of us is a person—a person with feelings and dreams and visions and goals.

Wasn't Carrie saying something profound? Of course, she was. She wanted to be known and loved and respected as a person. God does that for all of us. Shouldn't we do the same for one another?

How desolate life can be when people search for reasons or excuses for not liking one another. Isn't it much more pleasant to love than to hate, to give respect instead of dishonor? Jesus was the pacesetter in this regard. He called people by their names. No, he didn't deny that we have races, such as Jew, or Greek, or Samaritan, and neither should we. He didn't deny that some were poor, some rich, some male, some female, nor should we. He didn't allow these means of designation to depersonalize the individual. Neither should we. *Call me "Carrie"—that's my name.* What's yours?

Lord, thank you that to you we are not numbers—we are names. We are individuals with hopes and fears. We laugh, and we cry. Thank you for the significance you have given us by loving us and sending your Son to die for us. Amen.

John 1:47-48

God's Gifts

Hymn Suggestions: "Jesus Calls Us O'er the Tumult"; "I Need Thee Every Hour"

I shall never forget the expression on a little three-year-old's face when he found a colored egg in a community Easter egg hunt. There were several hundred eggs to be found, but there were scores of children looking for them.

There it was—a baby blue egg in a clump of grass. What excitement for a child! (Dad, too!) He found it himself, and he could keep it.

As we entered the car to head for home, he clutched the egg a little too tightly, and it broke. It really broke! Someone had failed to boil the egg, and there, over the back of the car seat, were the drippings of an egg. The child wept.

I wonder how many people do that with other matters in life. We search and search for life's treasures. Some of them are golden; dollar marks cover them. Some of them a multi-colored, rather exotic, or even erotic; they stimulate our senses. Some of them are rotten, but we don't know that because they're colored. We find them uncooked, and they break, and we're left with crushed shells in our hands.

God's gift of salvation is not that way. When you receive Christ, you know that no "egg of life" could ever satisfy your heart's hunger as he can. You might even say you have found "the pearl of greatest price." That's better than an egg, isn't it? Happy hunting!

Lord, all of us are seekers. We look for things in life that will bring us pleasure and satisfaction, but we're so easily fooled. We judge books by their covers and eggs by their shells. Help us discover your peace through faith in Jesus Christ. Amen.

Matthew 13:44-45

Could We Be Friends?

Hymn Suggestions: "I've Found a Friend";
                        "Trust and Obey"

Have you ever studied the facial expressions of a cat and a dog as they carefully move around each other? It's a fascinating experience to wonder what each might be thinking (if indeed they can think, which probably they cannot.)

Our small yellow cat seemed to say to our neighbor's little yellow dog, "Look Buster, we're about the same size, but I don't like your looks. We're different. Oh, I know we both have four legs, two eyes, and peculiar looking noses, although I happen to think my petite nose is cuter than your long snout. Besides that, your mouth is too big, and your voice is too gruff!"

And the dog must think, "What a queer looking thing you are, little ears. And why do you have to hump your back like that when I'm around?"

So I watch a little yellow cat and a little yellow dog take measure of each other. Sometimes I think they would like to play together. They might even learn to like each other and become close friends. I think that maybe the reason they don't is partly because they are suspicious of each other; they don't really know each other.

I wonder if you know any people who might be like that, suspicious, cautious, critical, analyzing every move and every word another might be saying. If we really tried, do you think we might become friends? I wonder.

Father, for all of us little creatures of yours who walk around on earth looking at one another from the corners of our eyes, forgive us. Help us not to judge another by any measurement other than your love. Make friends of enemies, we pray. Amen.

Philippians 4:2-4

God Never Lets Go

Hymn Suggestions: "My Faith Looks Up to Thee";
"O Love That Wilt Not Let Me Go"

Some time ago I had the privilege of walking across a swinging bridge with a friend walking ahead of me. As he tried to keep his balance, he said, "You know something, this thing is out of harmony. It doesn't meet your next step like it is supposed to." What he didn't know was that I was behind him giving a gentle bounce to my steps, forcing the homemade bridge to undulate beneath our feet.

Have you ever felt that life was not "meeting your feet" the way it is supposed to? Swinging bridges are anchored on each side of the chasm they span, but they are not anchored in the middle. Can life be that way, too? I think so.

Some people have good solid beginnings to life's journey. They were raised properly, and, perhaps, they will come back to their faith when life's journey is over. But in the middle of life it is easy for one to be somewhat "unanchored."

The psalmist said, "My feet had almost stumbled, my steps had nearly slipped. For I was envious of the arrogant when I saw the prosperity of the wicked (Ps. 73:2-3 MLB)." He was anchored in others, not in God. People may let us down. God won't.

There will always be people who bounce the bridge for us. We can fight back if we want to do so. But the people who seem to be able to walk successfully across the bridges of life are those who are holding to God's hand. Try that for a change.

Lord, when I feel the earth shaking beneath my feet, help me to stand firm on a foundation that cannot be shaken, the foundation of your love, of your Word, of your will. When others give me a hard time, teach me that retaliation is counterproductive. Through Christ, my Lord, amen.

II Timothy 2:18-19

Consider the Turtle

Hymn Suggestions: "Trusting Jesus";
"My Faith Looks Up to Thee"

The poor turtle, from fiction to fantasy, has been the recipient of more than its share of unfair attention. It is true that the turtle was the celebrated winner of the now-famous race with the rapid, but distracted, hare. But the turtle has been maligned by the criticism we level at people who are dawdlers in their pace. "Slow as a turtle," we say.

"Consider the turtle. He makes progress only when he sticks his neck out." That is true, but then he must take the risk of getting part of himself out of a shell. What about people who must take the same risk? People have shells, too, you know. We call them our privacies or inhibitions or other such names, but they're really shells.

Shells can be very comfortable. We can't be hurt badly while encased in a shell. But then, we can't experience the best of life, either.

Life was not meant to be lived in a shell—by a turtle or by a person. God meant for us to take risks; *faith* is the Bible's word. Faith really is a risk. We don't know for sure what it will bring.

People take risks on the stock market, the pleasure palaces, the horses, or even that which is bottled in bond. Why not take a risk on God? Why not have faith in God? Great people have been risk-takers. If you try to save your life, you'll lose it; so consider the turtle.

Lord, may I confess to you that I have a lot of security and comfort inside my shell—security, but not much excitement; security, but not much fulfillment. If I don't carry the ball, I won't make a fumble, will I? But Lord, I won't know the joy of scoring a touchdown either, will I? Help me to stick my neck out for you. Amen.

John 12:24

Taking Off Our Masks

Hymn Suggestions: "Blest Be the Tie";
"Leaning on the Everlasting Arms"

Each Halloween, I find myself nostalgically reflecting back to my own "trick or treat" days. Life was somewhat simpler then. For the most part, we made our own costumes, with the exception of the masks. With rolled-down grocery sacks, we embarked on our candy-seeking adventures."

The masks, or "false faces" as we called them, always intrigued me. I looked at the eyes of the person behind the mask and wondered if he or she were smiling or snarling, as the mask might have indicated. Was the person a friend or a foe?

Now that I am an adult, I still look at the masks, only they're different. They're real faces with real eyes, but they conceal the identities of the persons who wear them. People don't really want others to see them, so they wear faces that sometimes disguise their hearts.

Why do we do that? Paul Tournier said that we have a desire to be known, but a fear of being known. We want to take off our masks, but we're afraid we might get hurt by those who would not appreciate who we really are.

In the Christian faith, we must realize that God knows who we really are. What's more, he likes us. No, he loves us! And some Christians are learning to love and to accept people for who they are. We should try to find at least one of them and let that person get to know us. When you and I can find a person who accepts us as we are, it will be life's greatest treat; that's no trick.

Lord, I have a hunger to show my real self, to let someone see me as I really am. But I also have the fear that I would lose more than I would gain. Help me to find the freedom that I seek. Amen.

Isaiah 6:5-7

Starting Over . . . with God

Hymn Suggestions: "God of Grace and God of Glory";
"Where Cross the Crowded Ways of Life"

Starting over is an experience people will always have to face. From the beginning of time it has been so; people have had to face life in the light of significant changes that have altered life's patterns. They have had to begin again. For some, it has been as the result of a death or of a divorce. For some, it has come as the result of a departure, of children from the family nest or maybe of a parent who must leave to find work.

Starting over is with us in other ways, too. It has been estimated that the average young person entering the job market today will change jobs at least seven times before retirement. If one is to make this adjustment successfully, it will take a particular frame of mind and spirit. Mentally, we must accept the fact that few things stay the same. Spiritually, those who believe in God must rely on the resources of their faith.

God can work all things together for something good. He comforts us when we lose our loved ones. When our family nests are disturbed, it is God who can give fulfillment and peace.

If those who are forced to start over will surrender their new places, new experiences, and new circumstances to God, they will find that God can supply every need. Trust him.

Lord, when we feel the sand shifting beneath our feet, when some of those things we have learned to depend on are no longer dependable, when life changes, help us to anchor our souls in the great unchanging one—Jesus. Amen.

Romans 8:37-39

Waiting

Hymn Suggestions: "Footsteps of Jesus";
"Make Me a Blessing"

He didn't have much of a chance. He was smaller than the rest of them, and when they chose up sides for anything, he was either left out or taken as the one left over.

He had the uncanny ability to sleep on his hair the wrong way, so it seemed never to look very good. As hard as he tried, he could never rid his face of teenage blemishes.

When things went wrong in the classroom, the finger of suspicion pointed to him. After all, what better (or worse) person could you pick?

What people didn't realize was that the little guy hurt just like others, felt like others, hoped like others. But unlike most others, he was never treated as if he were like others.

Others received the valentines; he got the empty envelopes. Others begged one another to share a locker, but not the little guy. He just went on trying to keep from quitting, hoping that someday the tide would turn.

One day Jesus found one of those little guys up a tree. Jesus gave him some attention. Jesus called his name (they do have names, you know). Jesus gave a little guy hope.

I highly suspect that you and I might know one or two of these people who are waiting, waiting to be picked as a friend, waiting for their names to be called, waiting to be invited into our love and compassion.

Jesus said, "As you wish men would do to you, do so to them (Luke 6:31 RSV)." Good idea!

Lord, for all the little guys in the world, I pray that you will give them someone to love and to love them. Help them to feel a strong sense of your care and a keen awareness of care from others. Give them hope. Amen.

Luke 4:18-19

Rest in the Lord

Hymn Suggestions: "All the Way My Savior Leads Me";
"Standing on the Promises"

    A number of years ago a minister addressed a group of skid row derelicts in a downtown rescue mission. He knew some of them had been doctors, lawyers, teachers, and other highly respected leaders in their communities. He quoted to them from Rudyard Kipling's famous poem "If." Eloquently he moved through this gripping piece of poetry until he reached the lines: "If you can fill the unforgiving minute/With sixty seconds' worth of distance run." At that point, out of sheer desperation, one of the downtrodden men shouted, "Yes, but what if you can't? What if you try and still fail?"

    No doubt he voiced the sentiments of many people, people who are giving life their best shots and still seem to be coming up short. Some almost make it, but not quite. Some, like Moses of old, can see the land they hope to enter, but for some reason they fail to go in.

    Life poses some unanswered questions, and try as hard as we may, we cannot figure them out. We may become bitter. We may become hostile. Or we may rest our case in the hands of the Lord.

    Paul had the right frame of mind when he said, "Having done all, stand!" When you have given it your best, when you have genuinely tried, stand on your record. Keep your head up.

    Time will honor those of us who sincerely try—even if we fail.

Lord, none of us wants to fail. Help us to know that you expect us to do the best we can with what we have and to leave the results up to you. Knowing that you cannot fail, I trust my life into your care. Amen.

I Kings 8:17-19

Loneliness

Hymn Suggestions: "I Need Thee Every Hour";
"Lord, for Tomorrow and Its Needs"

Are you lonely? Many people are. Sometimes we think loneliness is contingent upon being alone, but that isn't necessarily so. Sometimes being alone allows a person the freedom to cry, to meditate, and to pray without worry of anyone's questioning why. Relief comes, a presence appears, and one is comforted.

On the other hand, crowds do not eliminate loneliness; sometimes they create it. We see people working and playing, laughing and praying, and if we haven't found a place in which we feel meaning and purpose, we only become lonelier still.

Sometimes people become lonely when they are uprooted from their known existence and thus become unknown. Changes can challenge us, but they can also produce loneliness.

Loneliness is eliminated, in part, when we are busy, but more so when we are known, loved, accepted, and can accept ourselves.

When Paul experienced loneliness in a Roman prison, he spoke of the absence of his friends. Then he said, "Notwithstanding the Lord stood with me, and strengthened me (II Tim. 4:17 KJV)." Loneliness was eliminated not by people, but by the deep, abiding presence of the Spirit of Christ.

If God cares about all the needs we have, then he cares about those times when we are deeply lonely. Talk to him about it; he's waiting to hear from you.

Lord, sometimes the world is a cold and lonely place. Sometimes it seems as if I have no true friends. Is it because others do not care? Is it because I haven't opened my life to them? Whatever the cause, Lord, I pray that you will help me—now. Amen.

Hebrews 13:5-6

Let Us Not Be Weary

Hymn Suggestions: "Savior, Like a Shepherd Lead Us"
"Savior, More Than Life to Me"

Most people are familiar with futility. We might call it by different names, but we know what it means.

To a fisherman, it is the casting of the line time after time and finding no fish.

To a farmer, it is the hope for rain to nourish starving crops, but day after day the sky remains blue.

To a teacher, it is the inability to impart knowledge to the mind of a student.

To an unemployed person, it is the filling out of one application after another, but receiving no phone call from an employer.

To a poor person, it is a matter of having too much month and not enough money.

To a laborer, it is having work that never gets done, but is only repeated in endless procession.

Futility is a fact of life for us all. Your futility will not be mine or mine yours. But everyone has some frustration. Is there a solution? There may not be a simple one. Sometimes we just have to keep on keeping on. Don't give up. Don't quit. Whatever your futility may be, be assured that God can help you in this area of your need. Turn your life over to him. Seek his guidance and strength. "Let us not be weary in well doing; for in due season, we shall reap, if we faint not" (Gal. 6:9 KJV).

Lord, I find it easy to want to throw up my hands and quit. Sometimes it seems as if all I do is beat my head against a brick wall. Help me not to quit until you do. Thank you for the strength you give. Amen.

II Corinthians 4:8-10

Let Go and Let God

Hymn Suggestions: "Jesus, Savior, Pilot Me";
"Lead, Kindly Light"

Mental depression is a terrible feeling. It saps our energy and prohibits us from functioning properly as human beings. Depression can be a product of many things. Weariness, physical illness, emotional let-downs, unrealistic expectations of ourselves and others—all of these can cause depression.

Maybe there is another reason for depression: divided loyalty. People who have a singular loyalty and commitment can proceed in life with a sense of direction and proper affection. Those who try to stand on two spots at one time have a divided mind.

Henry Drummond once said to a group of college students: "Gentlemen, I beseech you to seek the kingdom of God first or not at all. I promise you a miserable time if you seek it second."

When we are not fully committed to a singular loyalty, we must watch out for the demon of depression. When it comes, it may produce drug dependency, alcoholism, neuroses, or, in some cases, suicide.

Depression is a debilitating emotion. Maybe we are not wrong to feel depressed from time to time, but that isn't the way God would desire us to stay. Let him who is the Master of wind and waves become the Master of the tossing seas of our troubled minds and spirits.

Lord, when the sky seems so dark that it makes my whole world black, when the sun appears as if it will never shine again, when my insides feel as if they have dropped anchor in the bottomless pit, I pray that you will show me your face. Amen.

Matthew 6:24, 33

Get Well, Soon

Hymn Suggestions: "Jesus Saves";
"The Great Physician"

How do you handle those areas of the past in which you have suffered pain? Some people suppress them; they don't want to think about them. Others use their painful experiences as devices for getting sympathy. They wallow in self-pity and attempt to get compassionate responses from others.

Then there are those who treat their pain as a child might treat a cut on the finger. The child is aware of the injury and the pain the cut produces, but picks at it and, rather than promoting healing, prevents its healing. Not only that, but the child also runs the risk of creating an infection.

How do we make that mistake with other kinds of pain? For one thing, we talk too much about our problems, thus disallowing time, which is on God's side, to help heal our hurts. And as we proceed to probe and dwell on the issue, we tend to "infect" our thoughts and cause some emotional poison to set in.

We must learn to accept the reality of the painful event no matter how much it hurts. We must talk about it realistically, but then move on and allow God to bring about the healing we desire. Scars often remain as reminders, but the pain can be removed.

Remember that Christ is a Physician as well as the Savior. Let him do his work of healing you. Get well soon.

Lord, I confess my mixed emotions. Part of me wants to forget the pain, while another part keeps reminding me of it. Help me to get myself together on the side of healing. I trust you. Amen.

Matthew 11:28-30

God Is *for Us*

Hymn Suggestions: "Love, Mercy, and Grace"; "Love Divine"

I have often wondered what the worst form of punishment might be that people mete out to people. The electric chair? The firing squad? The gas chamber? The guillotine? Those are certainly awesome ways for society to tell a person, "We no longer want you among us."

We've heard about the floggings, the stocks where one became a public spectacle, and the brands which marked a woman as a scarlet lady, an adulteress during the Puritan era. But what about our era? In some societies, a lawbreaker is often placed in a room in which the ceiling was too low to stand erect, and the width was too narrow to stretch out the body to its full length. That is a horrible thought! Many of us are pretty good at punishing ourselves and others that way. We don't actually build rooms of those dimensions, but we limit ourselves and others in such a way as to induce emotional crippling.

How do we do it? By not allowing ourselves or others to grow, to stand tall. We inhibit people by demoralizing them with unending criticism. We fail to encourage the "bent over" person. We won't forgive ourselves when we have sinned and received God's forgiveness.

Through God's mercy and grace, we have been enabled to stand erect and say defiantly, "If God be for us, who can stand against us?" That's a good thought!

Lord, some of us have been bent over for a long time; we don't know how to stand tall. Thank you for raising the roof for us in Jesus Christ. Help us to make the room large enough for others, too. In Jesus' name, amen.

John 5:5-8

Comfort One Another

Hymn Suggestions: "God Is Love";
                       "Just When I Need Him Most"

The little lad was running fast when he fell and skinned his knee. It didn't look good, and he was crying, as well he should have been. His father chided him gently, "Son, stop that crying. You're O.K."

"But Daddy, it hurts so bad," the child said through his tears.

Why is it that we have such a difficult time with tears, especially the tears of another person? Is it because we have been taught to be strong and think tears belie that strength? Do we associate tears with weakness? When we can't take it any longer, we cry. But Jesus cried at the graveside of Lazarus, and he wasn't weak.

Is it because we have a hard time accepting the sadness and pain of another? Perhaps. We do feel helpless when we know that some unalterable event has happened to produce deep pain for another person.

Unfortunately, life has a lot of pain in it. People have physical suffering that pushes them into comatose, nonfeeling states. Others can hardly bear their agony. Some are mental sufferers; worries and anxieties overwhelm them.

The Bible teaches us that it is all right to need comfort. Comfort, encouragement, and genuine sympathy can enable another person to bear pain. Without comfort, we suffer alone. Had the father acknowledged the pain of the child and entered into the suffering with sympathy, he could have been an agent of healing. God does that for us, doesn't he?

Lord, I may not be able to cure the suffering of another, but help me not to be so callous as not to care. Teach me how to comfort as you have comforted all your children. In Jesus' name, amen.

Galatians 6:2

The Story of My Life

Hymn Suggestions: "Blessed Redeemer";
"I Love to Tell the Story"

Often someone will speak disparagingly of an adverse circumstance and say, "That's the story of my life."

Suppose you were asked to write the story of your life. How would you do it? No doubt some of us would write a story of loosely connected events, for many of us feel that life is like a steel ball in some giant pinball machine. The ball bounces from bumper to bumper, occasionally lands in a hole, is ejected, rings a bell here and there, and if it avoids being tilted, scores a few points, and then drops harmlessly into the place of all spent steel balls—the grave at the bottom.

Others see more meaning and purpose to life. We have goals and ambitions that follow a carefully planned agenda. We experience some disappointments along the way, but at least we measure our success by the degree to which our achievements have equaled our plans.

Have you ever heard of Anne Sullivan? Many people haven't, at least not as many as have heard of Helen Keller. Helen Keller was born without sight or hearing. Anne Sullivan entered her life and, through the language of touch, was able to communicate sight and sound. Later in Miss Keller's life, one of her books bore this tribute: "To Anne Sullivan, whose love is the story of my life."

The best tribute we can give is this: "To Jesus Christ, whose love is the story of my life." He makes life worth living.

And so, Lord, we go on living because we know that you will go on loving, forgiving, helping, and healing. Your love truly is the story of our lives. Lord, may our love be such that others will want to know your story. Amen.

Ephesians 2:4-5

Friend or Enemy?

Hymn Suggestions: "Awake, My Soul";
                       " 'Tis So Sweet to Trust in Jesus"

As a boy growing up in West Virginia, I wanted to make some spending money for myself. So I tried selling flower seeds, greeting cards, the *Grit* newspaper, Cloverine salve, and finally, I became a newsboy selling the morning and evening newspapers.

The thing I disliked most about my job was that it interfered with my sleep in the morning and my play in the afternoon. I also disliked dealing with the dogs. I never really learned how to handle them. I tried rocks, sticks, a water pistol, a flashlight in the mornings, and a gruff voice. But how gruff can a thirteen-year-old boy, whose voice is in the process of changing, sound?

A few years ago I heard about a letter carrier who also had to deal with the dogs. Instead of hitting them or threatening them or running from them, he decided to feed them. He carried a box of dog food and fed about eighteen dogs a day. I either made enemies of the dogs or, at best, kept my distance. He made friends.

Maybe there is a lesson to be learned in that. Life is filled with people who threaten us in one way or another. We can deal violently with them, scream at them, or ignore them. Could we not learn to "feed" them?

The best way to get rid of an enemy is to make a friend of that person. We can keep fighting if we desire, but God has asked us to make friends of our enemies. Are you ready to try?

Lord, we know how we're supposed to treat those who abuse us. Knowing what to do is not our problem. We find it easier to reject them and even to retaliate against them than to love them. Give us the mind of Christ. Amen.

Romans 12:17-18

A Meaningful Life

Hymn Suggestions: "More About Jesus";
"I Would Be True"

Albert Schweitzer once said that the supreme tragedy in life is outliving yourself. That can happen whenever we live longer than we want to, when our zest for life has died, and when we no longer think of each day as a fresh, new adventure.

Boredom is one of the peculiar diseases of our age. People who do nothing more than mark their days off on a calendar in uselessness become both bored and bores. Because they see no real captivating and exciting meaning in life, they scowl and accuse.

Life has a depth and dimension that many of us have never realized. There is so much to do, so much that needs to be done. We can find value in many worthwhile ventures if we only want to do so.

If you spend all your time looking at the ground, you'll never see the sunrise or the sunset, you'll never see the smile that creases an aged face or the twinkle in the eye of a child. And what's more, you'll develop a grumpy disposition, a hateful attitude, a bitter spirit, and, as Schweitzer said, you'll probably still be living a long time after your life and its meaning have ended.

Bitter people drive others away from them and are left with their reward—themselves. Now wouldn't it be better to live for God and others? I think so; I hope you do, too.

Lord, while it is true that there is enough in life to discourage the most optimistic of people, help us to know that there are enough opportunities, enough strength from you and your Word to enable us to live to the fullest all of our days. Make us givers and not takers. Amen.

Philippians 1:21-25

"Likes" from "Lacks"

Hymn Suggestions: "Since Jesus Came into My Heart"; "He Keeps Me Singing"

An architect who helped design a beautiful city in an Arizona desert said that the architecture of an area is determined by the lack of available materials. Life is somewhat like that, isn't it? If we were given the privilege of choosing the materials we would use in fashioning a body, no doubt we would choose nothing but the best. We would choose good health, beauty, ability, dexterity, and strength. Who would choose blindness over sight or deafness over hearing? Who would choose to be lame while others could walk and run?

Yet, we must build our lives from the "lacks" and not from the "likes." We must, if we are to enjoy life, learn how best to employ the materials that are available.

The most unhappy people are those who complain about what they do not have. People who become bitter and resentful because others seem to have more are seldom life's cherished companions.

If an architect can make a city beautiful from the "lacks," surely God enables us to do the same with our lives. We must be alert to the possibilities and blessings that are available.

Jesus took a hillside and made it a sacred place. He took a grave and made it a doorway into the Father's house. He made "likes" out of "lacks." We can, too.

Lord, life would be much easier if everything were tailor-made to lead to happiness. Help us to know that the real beauty of life is not in its sameness, but in its difference. Thank you for being more concerned about the builder than the materials. Help us to build beautiful lives. Amen.

II Corinthians 12:7-9

God's Enabling Love

Hymn Suggestions: "O Love That Wilt Not Let Me Go"; "Love Is the Theme"

Getting along with everyone in this life just might be an impossibility. Maybe it's not really "impossible", but let's say highly improbable.

Will Rogers is quoted as having said, "I never met a man I didn't like." Most of us can't say that. There are many reasons why we dislike some people.

We dislike those who are threats to us, to our patterns of thought, to our philosophies, or to our positions in life. Those who create insecurity for us often arouse our hostility.

We dislike those who hurt us or who hurt those we love. It isn't easy to appreciate someone who deliberately and maliciously causes us to have pain.

We sometimes dislike those who make us feel guilty. Perhaps their life-styles are superior to ours, or maybe they do to us what Jesus seemed to do to his crucifiers—threaten us with goodness.

The most inexcusable of our dislikes are those of facial features, of tones of voice, of personality types, and of persons we don't even know. Life is too short, too complex, too difficult for us to carry the added burden of hatred. God has asked us to love.

Jesus had a good idea. He said for us to do good to those who hate us and to pray for those who despitefully use us. That may be hard to do, but it's the right thing to do. What God commands, he makes possible. He enables us to love.

Lord, I confess there are some people I don't like. I don't like the way they act, the way they treat others, or the way they treat me. I really don't want to like those people. Forgive me, Father, and help me to learn to like them. Amen.

I John 4:7-8

Self-appreciation

Hymn Suggestions: "My Jesus, I Love Thee";
"Savior, Teach Me Day by Day"

Why is it that so many people would like to be somebody else? Is it because other people look better, act better, feel better, think better, or have better positions in life? Perhaps they do. But then, many people might think those same things about us.

Self-appreciation is a difficult commodity to come by. It is true that some people have self-confidence and self-appreciation, but there is an epidemic of inferiority going around.

If we are not pretty or greatly intelligent or rich or the head of the company, then forget it! We are not worth much, so we are told by life. The sad part is that we often believe it.

If you are a self-hater, how do you get out of that miserable condition? Consider God's love for you as a place to start. He made you to be one of a kind. Jesus died for you. The biblical appraisal of [humankind] is that we are made just a little lower than the angels.

To hate oneself is to show a lack of understanding of what God can do in and through one's life. Everything that has happened to any of us may not be good, but God can use us and those experiences to make life good.

Maybe when we accept God's love and his place for us, we'll learn to accept ourselves, too. Believe me—that is one of life's best gifts—to appreciate oneself.

Lord, the next time I say I am not worth much, help me to get a fresh glimpse of the cross. Scream at me, if you must, and tell me I am insulting you. But Lord, would you do me a special favor? Use someone important to me to tell me how much I really am worth. Thank you. Amen.

Jeremiah 1:4-7

Making Decisions

Hymn Suggestions: "A Child of the King";
"It Is Well with My Soul"

While interviewing a person for possible employment, the agency manager mentioned an opening in Florida. "But can you pick lemons?" he asked. Quickly the applicant responded, "Boy, can I! I've been married five times."

For some people, that's where their talent seems to lie; they are adept at making bad choices. "I never seem to do the right thing!" the anguished cry.

Decision-making is seldom an easy task, particularly when it comes to those heavy areas of life—choosing a mate, employment, a life-style, beliefs, and so forth. How can we make it easier for ourselves?

First, we must find a standard by which to measure our choices. For some, the standard is money. For others, it might be power or prestige. For still others, it might be the realm of feelings, pampering and pleasing the body.

How about God's will? But how can we know God's will? Perhaps other questions need to be asked: Will the world be a better place because of what I am doing? Is it for the good of others? Am I gifted in the area of this need?

Second, in making decisions we must look beyond the immediate moment and consider the larger picture. If I follow this road, where will it eventually lead?

Third, we must accept the fact that even good decisions take work for them to benefit us and others. Good decisions can be made. Trust God and see.

Lord, I want to make the right decisions. I have experienced pain from wrong decisions. Please help me to use your standard of measurement, and then, Lord, help me to have the strength to see it through. Amen.

Jeremiah 6:16

Are You Listening?

Hymn Suggestions: "Just When I Need Him Most"; "Lead Me to Calvary"

"Henry, you're not listening to me!" Henry takes another sip of black coffee (better for the waistline, you know) and continues to read the morning paper. His wife seethes with anger, and he thrives on apathy.

Listening is difficult for some of us to do. Sometimes we are preoccupied with other thoughts, and we don't concentrate on what the speaker is saying. Sometimes our interests are vastly different.

Yet, it is extremely important for us to try to be good listeners. People will talk to those who will listen. When our questions, hurts, fears, and needs are not heard by the one who is significant to us, we sometimes search for another one who will listen. That is not always good for us. It has caused children to get mixed up with the wrong crowd. It has caused husbands and wives to become infatuated with other people.

Good listening involves time, attention, eye contact, and response. That response need not always be advice. Sometimes sympathy and understanding will do very well.

Jesus was a good listener. He knew how to make the speaker feel important. He concentrated on what was being said. He enabled children to feel as if he really cared for them, because he really did. Jesus knew that real listening indicated unselfishness, care, and genuine love. Are you a good listener? Are you listening now?

Lord, I confess that too often I am more interested in what I am saying, or want to say, than to what you are trying to say to me. Help me to hear your words first and then to listen to the words of others. Amen.

Mark 7:37

Blessed Interruptions

Hymn Suggestions: "I Would Be True";
"O Young and Fearless Prophet"

"Don't you interrupt me!"

We say that all the time, don't we? We say it because we are always being interrupted by someone, or so it seems. We move routinely through our days, weeks, and years of life, but now and then sickness, accidents, death, and other unwanted intruders break into our lives and interrupt our peace.

Some people are interrupted by the loss of an occupation or by a move to a new city or by some change in situation. New schools, neighborhoods, churches, friends—all of these become, in some way, our interruptions.

What if life never had any interruptions? What if everything just cruised along? Would that be better for us? Sometimes we think we would like that very much; sometimes we need extended periods of time in which that is true. But the truth of the matter is that we do need interruptions.

Some of the best things in life have been unplanned. An interruption has put us in touch with a person or with an event that has literally changed the course of life for us.

Jesus was interrupted many times, but he did not count the interruptions as lost time. He made them opportunities in which he could help another person. So why lose time complaining about interruptions? Wouldn't it be better to look for constructive ways of handling them? Your disappointment could become an appointment . . . with God.

Slow me down, Lord, even if you have to use interruptions. I miss so much of life that I need to see. Teach me how to use my interruptions as opportunities for honoring your Son and for helping others. In Jesus' name, I pray, amen.

Acts 16:7-9

Under Our Skin

Hymn Suggestions: "Open My Eyes That I May See"; "More Like Jesus"

In Harper Lee's novel *To Kill a Mockingbird*, Atticus says, "If you can learn a simple trick, you'll get along a lot better with all kinds of folks. You never really understand a person until you climb into his skin and walk around in it."

What is it like to get inside the skin of another person? How can we do that? For one thing, we can try to put ourselves in the position of the other person. We can let our minds dwell on his or her set of circumstances. We can struggle with the struggles, feel the rocks in the shoes, and experience the pinch of the tight adversities.

It is easy for us to prejudge another person. We base much of our appraisal on circumstantial evidence, outward appearances; these might be isolated actions of those whom we criticize and reject.

The beauty of Jesus is that he lived for thirty-three years in human skin. That gave him a proper understanding of our weaknesses, temptations, and suffering. Maybe that is why God is more patient than we are. "He remembers our frame that we are dust." Knowing that, he deals with us patiently, lovingly, and acceptingly. Thus he is able to make us into something better for his kingdom's sake.

When you and I really allow Jesus to get under our skin, we'll find it easier to get inside the skin of others, and less often will they irritate and offend us.

Lord, thank you for the time you entered human skin. I know it was a humbling thing to do, but I feel much better in knowing that you know first-hand what I'm going through. Help me to be more tolerant of and helpful to others whose lives may be in deep pain. Amen.

Hebrews 4:15-16

A Little Kinder Than Necessary

Hymn Suggestions: "Open My Eyes That I May See"; "So Let Our Lips and Lives Express"

In J. M. Barrie's play *Little White Bird* a young husband waits at the hospital for his child to be born. He has never been unkind to his wife, but he wonders if he has been as kind as he might have been. "Let us make a rule from tonight," he says, "always to be a little kinder than necessary."

"A little kinder than necessary"—what would our homes, our churches, our politics, our world be like if everyone practiced that philosophy? Part of the answer depends on our concept of *necessary kindness*. To some, necessary kindness is conditional: "I'll be kind to you if you'll be kind to me"; "I'll speak to you if you'll speak to me"; "I'll smile at you if you'll smile at me."

When Abraham Lincoln's friends urged him to make a stinging reply to a bitter, untrue word spoken about him, he said, "Somehow, I never thought it paid." And it doesn't!

So many relationships suffer pain and agony because of unkindness. Evil deeds breed evil deeds. Negative replies beget negative responses. *A little kinder than necessary*—that's what we need if we are going to create deeper friendships, preserve more marriages, and make life better for everyone.

Anyone can be negative and unkind. In fact, most people can be kind to someone who is kind. *A little kinder than necessary.* That's what we really need, isn't it?

Lord, when I think of all the hurting people, help me learn to be kind. Make my kindness like your kindness, unconditional and overflowing. Help me to look beyond the faults of others to see their needs. Amen.

Luke 6:30-32